THE OWL AND THE PUSSYCAT
AND OTHER POEMS

By EDWARD LEAR

Illustrated by MARGARET JERVIS

The Owl and the Pussycat and Other Poems
By Edward Lear
Illustrated by Margaret Jervis

Print ISBN 13: 978-1-4209-7441-6
eBook ISBN 13: 978-1-4209-7445-4

Cover Image: a reproduction of the original cover illustration, first published by Avon Publications, New York, c. 1953.

Please visit *www.digireads.com*

the **OWL** and

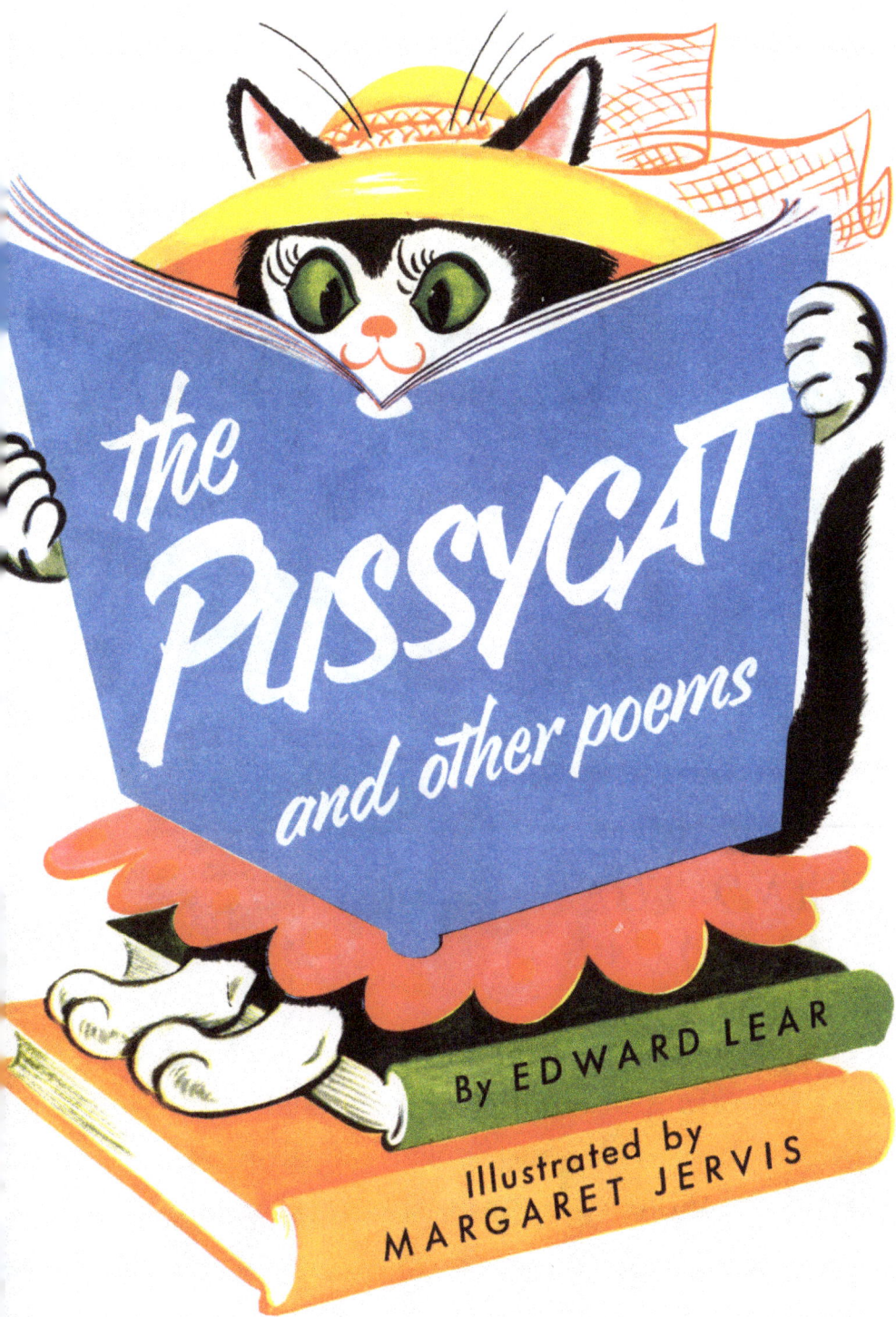

the PUSSYCAT
and other poems

BY EDWARD LEAR

Illustrated by
MARGARET JERVIS

THE OWL
AND THE
PUSSYCAT

The Owl and the Pussycat went to sea
In a beautiful pea-green boat.
They took some honey, and plenty of money
Wrapped up in a five-pound note.

The Owl looked up to the stars above,
And sang to a small guitar,
"O lovely Pussy, O Pussy, my love,
What a beautiful Pussy you are,
You are, you are,
What a beautiful Pussy you are!"

Pussy said to the Owl, "You elegant fowl,
   How charmingly sweet you sing!
Oh, let us be married; too long we have tarried!
   But what shall we do for a ring?"

They sailed away, for a year and a day,
　　To the land where the bong tree grows;
And there in a wood a Piggywig stood,
　　With a ring at the end of his nose,
　　　　His nose, his nose,
　　With a ring at the end of his nose.

"Dear Pig, are you willing to sell for one shilling
    Your ring?" Said the Piggy, "I will."
So they took it away, and were married next day
    'By the Turkey who lives on the hill.

They dined on mince and slices of quince,
Which they ate with a runcible spoon;
And hand in hand, on the edge of the sand,
They danced by the light of the moon,
The moon, the moon,
They danced by the light of the moon.

THE POBBLE
WHO HAS
NO TOES

The Pobble who has no toes
   Had once as many as we;
When they said, "Some day you may lose them all,"
   He replied, "Fish fiddle-de-dee!"
And his Aunt Jobiska made him drink
Lavender water tinged with pink,
For she said, "The world in general knows
There's nothing so good for a Pobble's toes!"

The Pobble who has no toes
   Swam across the Bristol Channel;
But before he set out he wrapped his nose
   In a piece of scarlet flannel.
For his Aunt Jobiska said, "No harm
Can come to his toes if his nose is warm;
And it's perfectly known that a Pobble's toes
Are safe—provided he minds his nose."

The Pobble swam fast and well,
    And when boats or ships came near him,
He tinkledy-binkledy-winkled a bell
    So that all the world could hear him.

And all the Sailors and Admirals cried,
When they saw him nearing the farther side–
"He has gone to fish for his Aunt Jobiska's
Runcible Cat with crimson whiskers!"

But before he touched the shore—
   The shore of the Bristol Channel—
A sea-green Porpoise carried away
   His wrapper of scarlet flannel.
And when he came to observe his feet,
Formerly garnished with toes so neat,
His face at once became forlorn
On perceiving that all his toes were gone!

And nobody ever knew,
  From that dark day to the present,
Whoso had taken the Pobble's toes,
  In a manner so far from pleasant.
Whether the shrimps or crawfish gray,
Or crafty Mermaids stole them away,
Nobody knew; and nobody knows
How the Pobble was robbed of his twice five toes!

The Pobble who has no toes
    Was placed in a friendly bark,
And they rowed him back, and carried him up
    To his Aunt Jobiska's park.

And she made him a feast, at his earnest wish,
Of eggs and buttercups fried with fish;
And she said, "It's a fact the whole world knows
That Pobbles are happier without their toes."

THE QUANGLE WANGLE'S HAT

On the top of the Crumpetty Tree
The Quangle Wangle sat,
But his face you could not see,
On account of his Beaver Hat.

For his Hat was a hundred and two feet wide,
With ribbons and bibbons on every side,
And bells, and buttons, and loops, and lace,
So that nobody ever could see the face
    Of the Quangle Wangle Quee.

The Quangle Wangle said
   To himself on the Crumpetty Tree,
"Jam, and jelly, and bread
   Are the best of food for me!
But the longer I live on this Crumpetty Tree
The plainer than ever it seems to me
That very few people come this way,
And that life on the whole is far from gay!"
    Said the Quangle Wangle Quee.

But there came to the Crumpetty Tree
    Mr. and Mrs. Canary;
And they said, "Did ever you see
    Any spot so charmingly airy?
May we build a nest on your lovely Hat?
Mr. Quangle Wangle, grant us that!
O please let us come and build a nest
Of whatever material suits you best,
        Mr. Quangle Wangle Quee!"

And besides, to the Crumpetty Tree
    Came the Stork, the Duck, and the Owl;
The Snail and the Bumblebee,
    The Frog and the Fimble Fowl

(The Fimble Fowl, with a Corkscrew leg).
And all of them said, "We humbly beg
We may build our homes on your lovely Hat—
Mr. Quangle Wangle, grant us that!
    Mr. Quangle Wangle Quee!"

And the Golden Grouse came there,
And the Pobble who has no toes,
And the small Olympian Bear,
And the Dong with a luminous nose.

And the Blue Baboon who played the flute,
And the Orient Calf from the Land of Tute,
And the Attery Squash, and the Bisky Bat—
All came and built on the lovely Hat
    Of the Quangle Wangle Quee.

And the Quangle Wangle said
  To himself on the Crumpetty Tree,
"When all these creatures move
  What a wonderful noise there'll be!"

And at night by the light of the Mulberry Moon
They danced to the flute of the Blue Baboon,
On the broad green leaves of the Crumpetty Tree,
And all were as happy as happy could be,
    With the Quangle Wangle Quee.

www.ingramcontent.com/pod-product-compliance
Lightning Source LLC
Chambersburg PA
CBHW071807020426
42331CB00008B/2420